108 Quotes

on

NATURE

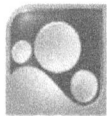

108 QUOTES ON NATURE

Published by:
    Amrita Books
    Amritapuri, Kollam Dt., Kerala
    INDIA 690525
    Email: inform@amritapuri.org
    Website: www.amritapuri.org

First edition: April 2015

Copyright © 2015 by Amrita Books, Amritapuri, Kollam

All rights reserved. No part of this publication may be stored in a retrieval system, transmitted, reproduced, transcribed or translated into any language, in any form, by any means without the prior agreement and written permission of the publisher.

Cover design from a painting by Vimal.

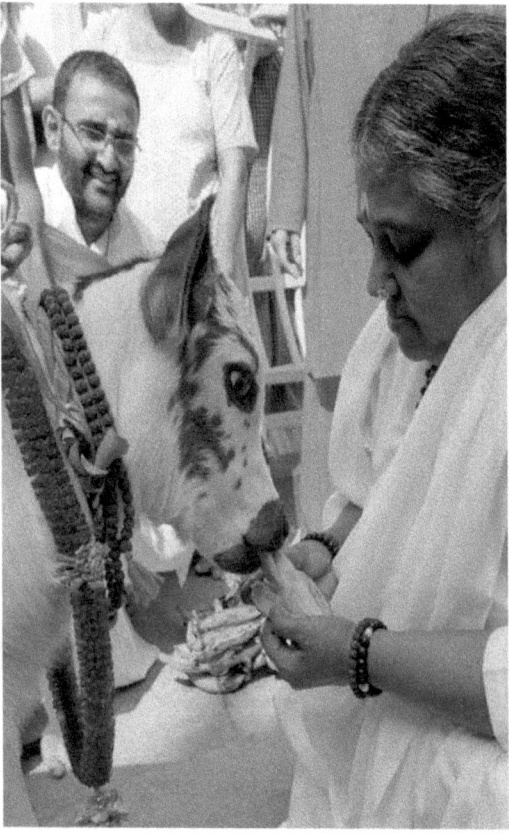

1

Nature is God's visible form that we can see and experience through our senses. By loving and serving nature, we are worshipping God directly. Let us try to reawaken this attitude.

2

There is one truth that shines through all of creation. God is the Pure Consciousness that dwells in everything. Rivers, mountains, plants, animals, the sun, moon and stars, you and I... are all expressions of this one Reality. It is by assimilating this truth into our lives, and thus gaining a deeper understanding, that we can discover the inherent beauty in diversity.

3

Our true nature is like the sky, not the clouds. Our true nature is like the ocean, not the waves. Clouds and waves come and go. The sky and the ocean remain.

4

Nature is an indispensable part of life on Earth. Everything relies on nature to live. We are not different from nature; we are an interdependent part of it. Our lives depend on the well being of the whole. Therefore, it is one of our foremost duties to lovingly care for all living things.

5

See how easily nature overcomes obstacles. If there is a stone in the path of a tiny ant, the ant just walks around the stone and continues on its way. If there is a rock where a tree is growing, the tree simply grows around the rock. In the same way, a river flows around a log that is blocking its path. We, too, should learn to adapt to all the circumstances in life, overcoming them with patience and enthusiasm.

6

When we find harmony within ourselves, it will benefit nature and be reflected throughout creation. When we do not have mental harmony, nature's harmony is also lost. For example, in many places around the world today, there is either too much rain or not enough; this is a reflection of our own disharmony in nature. Once the human mind is harmonised, the harmony of nature will spontaneously take place. Where there is concentration, there is harmony.

7

In a perfect relationship between humanity and nature, a circular energy field is created in which each flows into the other. To put it another way, when we human beings fall in love with nature, she will fall in love with us. She will stop hiding things from us. Opening her infinite treasure of wealth, she will allow us to enjoy it. Like a mother, she will protect, nurture and nourish us.

8

Nature is our first mother. She nurtures us throughout our lives. Our birth mother may allow us to sit on her lap for a couple of years, but Mother Nature patiently bears our weight for our entire lives. She sings us to sleep, feeds us and caresses us. Just as children are obligated to their birth mother, we should all feel an obligation and responsibility towards Mother Nature. If we forget this responsibility, it is equal to forgetting our own self.

9

Shouldn't we express our gratitude to Mother Earth, who patiently provides her lap for us to run, jump and play upon? Shouldn't we be grateful to the birds who sing for us, the flowers that blossom for us, the trees that provide shade for us and the rivers that flow for us?

10

One factor that connects human beings to nature is our innate innocence within. When we see a rainbow or the waves of the sea, do we still feel the innocent joy of a child? Look at the beauty of nature with the awareness that these are all unique expressions of the Divine.

11

There are no mistakes in God's creation. Every creature and every object that has been created by God is so utterly special.

Everything in nature is a wonderful miracle. Isn't a little bird flying through the vast sky a miracle? Isn't a tiny fish swimming in the depths of the ocean a miracle?

13

There are certain things in life that awaken enthusiasm and freshness whenever we think about or experience them, for example, the sea. No matter how many times we look at the sea, we never feel it's enough. There is an aspect of eternity in the sea. It's the same with the sky. The bond we feel towards nature is like this. We can always see newness in it.

14

Everything is pervaded by consciousness. This consciousness sustains the world and all creatures in it. To worship everything—seeing God in all—is what religion advises. Such an attitude teaches us to love nature. Think of the miracles of nature. Camels are blessed with a special bag to store water. The kangaroo has a cradle to carry its baby wherever it goes. Even the most insignificant and seemingly harmful creatures or plants have a specific use. Spiders keep the insect population in balance, snakes keep the rodent population under control and even the tiny, one-celled plankton in the ocean serve as food for whales. They each have a part of their own to play.

15

There is a rhythm to everything in the cosmos. The wind, the rain, the waves, the flow of our breath and heartbeat—everything has a rhythm. Similarly, there is a rhythm in life. Our thoughts and actions create the rhythm and melody. When the rhythm of our thoughts is lost, it reflects in our actions. This will, in turn, throw off the rhythm of life itself. Today, that is what we are seeing all around us.

16

Life is filled with God's light, but only through optimism will you experience that light. Look at the optimism of nature. Nothing can stop it. Every aspect of nature tirelessly contributes its share to life. The participation of a little bird, an animal, a tree or a flower is always complete. No matter what the hardships, they continue to try wholeheartedly.

17

Enjoy the beauty of nature with the awareness that this is all an expression of the Divine.

18

Stars are twinkling in the sky, rivers are flowing blissfully, branches of the trees are dancing in the wind, and birds are bursting into song. You should ask yourself, "Why do I feel so miserable living in the midst of all this joyful celebration?"

19

Flowers, stars, rivers, trees and birds do not have an ego; and being egoless, nothing can hurt them. Being egoless, you can only rejoice. Even occasions that would normally be painful are transformed into moments of joy.

20

Just as nature creates the favourable circumstances for a coconut to become a coconut tree, and for a seed to transform itself into a huge fruit tree, nature creates the necessary circumstances through which the individual soul can reach the Supreme Being and merge in eternal union.

21

Nature is a textbook from which we must learn. Each object in nature is a page of the textbook. Every object in nature teaches us something. Renunciation and selflessness are the greatest lessons that we can learn from nature.

22

Nature gives all of her wealth to human beings. Just as nature graciously serves, protects and helps us, it is our responsibility to return that dedication and service by helping her. Only then can the harmony between nature and humanity be preserved.

23

When we live harmoniously with nature in love and unity, we will have the strength to overcome any crisis.

24

Human beings can learn many things from nature. Look at an apple tree. It gives shade even to the person who cuts it down. It also gives all of its sweet, delicious fruit, keeping nothing for itself. Its very existence is for other living beings. Likewise, everyone comes and bathes in a river. The river washes away everyone's dirt, expecting nothing. It willingly accepts all impurities and returns purity, sacrificing everything for others. Children, each and every object in creation teaches us sacrifice.

25

Look at the charm of nature. Look at this amazing cosmos and the harmonious way in which our planet and all other planets function. The vast pattern of beauty and order that pervade creation makes it very clear that there is a big heart and great intelligence behind everything. Without a cosmic intelligence, a Universal Power that controls everything, how could such perfect order and beauty exist?

26

Creation is not accidental—the sun, moon, ocean, trees, flowers, mountains and valleys are not accidents. Planets move around the sun without straying even an inch from their predetermined orbits. The oceans cover vast areas of the globe, without swallowing up the earth. If this beautiful creation were simply accidental, it would not be so orderly and systematic.

27

The resolve of the Supreme Being is behind everything—behind the blossoming of a flower, the chirping of a bird, the movement of the wind, and the flames of a fire. It is the power by which everything grows, the power that sustains everything. That Divine resolve is the underlying cause of the birth, growth and death of all living beings. It is the cause of the entire creation. The power of the Supreme Being sustains the world. Without this power, the world would cease to exist.

28

The scriptures say, "Isavasyamidam Sarvam": everything is permeated with God-consciousness. The earth, trees, plants and animals are all manifestations of God. As this is so, we must have love and concern for nature as well as for each other.

29

When we, out of our innate innocence, believe in a Supreme Being and are filled with devotion, we will see the Divine in everything—in every tree and animal, in every aspect of nature. This attitude enables us to live in perfect harmony and in tune with nature.

30

Praying with concentration will restore the lost harmony of nature. Even if no one is there to hear it, Mother Nature keeps a record of each of our sincere prayers.

31

In truth, the progress and prosperity of humanity depend solely on the good that people do for nature. By establishing a loving bond between humanity and nature, we ensure both the balance of nature and the progress of humanity.

32

It is the urgent duty of all human beings to please nature by performing selfless actions endowed with love, faith, and sincerity. When this is done, nature will bless us back with abundance.

33

It is wrong to waste due to our lack of care and attention. Every object has been created to be used; every object in creation has a definite purpose.

34

Humanity is dependent on nature for its very existence. In truth, we are not protecting nature—it is nature who protects us.

35

Nature sacrifices herself for humans whereas we not only exploit her, but destroy her. Yet nature serves us.

36

In the old days, there was no particular need for environmental preservation because protecting nature was part of worshipping God and life itself. More than remembering "God," people used to love and serve nature and society. They saw the Creator through the creation. They loved, worshipped and protected nature as the visible form of God.

37

Mother Earth is serving us; the sun, the moon and the stars all serve us. What can we do in return for their selfless service?

38

When science advances, cities and business enterprises grow in tandem. As human population in cities increases, the amount of waste also increases exponentially. Therefore, we should discover scientific means for properly handling this waste. If not, our natural environment will decay and diseases will spread. We must strive as much as possible to recycle and reuse 'waste.' Mother Nature has her own miraculous ways of recycling and reusing waste, thus preserving life. Let it be our aim to create a world with zero waste.

39

We need to take up efforts to instil values in our children at a young age. We must teach them to love one another. We should fill the syllabuses of our schools and colleges with lessons about love and compassion and help put an end to the exploitation of the downtrodden. If we do this, war and violent clashes will lessen and, to some extent, we will be able to realise the dream of world peace. When mutual love grows, nature also will become peaceful.

40

Look at the beauty of nature. Living harmoniously with nature will in itself bring happiness and contentment.

41

The current generation lives as if it has no relationship with nature. Everything around us is artificial. Today, we eat fruit and grains grown with artificial fertilisers and pesticides. We add preservatives to increase their shelf life. Like this, consciously or unconsciously, we are continuously eating poison. As a result, many new diseases are appearing. In fact, long ago, the average life span was more than 100. But today people live only 80 years or less and more than 75 percent of the population will suffer from some disease or another.

42

Wanting more produce often prompts the use of artificial fertilizers and pesticides. It is because of this greed that we forget to love the plants. A balloon can be inflated only up to a limit, after that, if you keep blowing air into it, it will burst. Likewise, a seed has a certain limit to the yield it can give. If we keep trying to increase the yield by the use of artificial means, it will adversely affect the strength and quality of the seed and also do harm to those who eat it.

43

By harming plants, you are lengthening their karma. Your selfishness blocks their evolution into a higher species of life and prevents them from attaining eternal freedom.

44

Scientific inventions are highly beneficial, but they should not go against nature. Science has reached unimaginable heights but, unfortunately, we have lost the clarity to see the whole truth of things and to act with discrimination. A scientist should be a real lover—a lover of mankind, a lover of all creation and a lover of life.

45

As our selfishness increases, we become estranged from nature and begin to exploit her. Using nature for our needs is acceptable but taking more than what we need changes the circumstances and becomes exploitation. We must remember that when we take more than we need, we are destroying the life of that extra plant or animal.

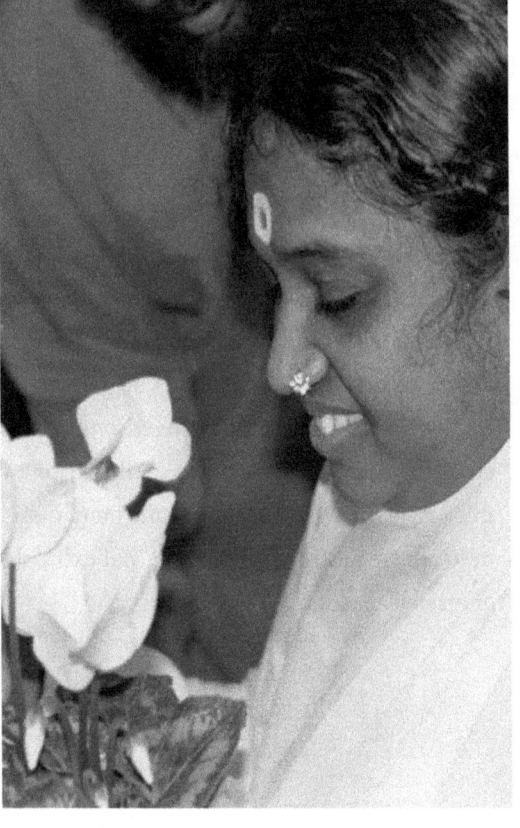

46

Look at the beauty and perfection of nature. Nature is so joyful, even though it doesn't have the intelligence of a human being. All of creation is rejoicing. A flower has a short life span, yet it offers itself wholeheartedly to others. It offers its own nectar to the bees—and this brings happiness.

47

Mother Earth is exploited, regardless of the wonderful boons and gifts she bestows upon us. Still, Mother Earth patiently bears everything and blesses humanity with immense wealth and prosperity.

48

Out of God's all-consuming love and compassion, She instructs and inspires all beings of the Earth to be patient and compassionate to humans, even though humans do not return their love.

49

Never satisfied, and in their greed to achieve and possess more, human beings have been doing all kinds of crooked actions that are polluting and exploiting Mother Nature. Steeped in selfishness, people have forgotten that it was from Mother Nature that we have received everything—and without her, we will lose everything.

50

According to Sanatana Dharma, the eternal religion, nature is not different from human beings. There is a mantra we chant every day, "Lokah Samastah Sukhino Bhavantu," which means, let there be peace and happiness for all beings in all the worlds. It includes all of nature, the whole plant and animal kingdoms, and the entire creation. To see oneness in diversity is what Sanatana Dharma teaches us and is the essence of this mantra.

51

Nature is a huge flower garden. Animals, birds, trees, plants and people are the garden's fully blossomed flowers of diverse colours. The beauty of this garden is complete only when all of these exist in unity, thereby spreading the vibrations of love and oneness. Let us work together to prevent these diverse flowers from withering away, so that the garden may remain eternally beautiful.

52

Modern science says that trees and plants respond to the thoughts and actions of human beings. Scientists have created instruments that can detect and register the feelings of plants and, in some cases, even measure the intensity of such feelings. They have observed that, through loveless actions and lack of compassion, plants also suffer. Ages ago, the saints and sages of India, having understood this great truth, lived a life of complete harmlessness.

53

Nature is like a goose that lays golden eggs. If we think that we can claim all the golden eggs for ourselves by killing the goose, the result will be total destruction for humanity. For our own survival and the survival for the coming generations, we have to stop polluting and exploiting nature.

54

Human beings, through their ego-centered thoughts and actions, have polluted the atmosphere. The atmosphere is completely filled with poisonous smoke and gases from cars, buses and factories, but the worst poison that pollutes the atmosphere is the selfish and wicked thoughts of human beings.

55

Only through love and respect of nature will we become spiritually awakened. Our goal is to feel life everywhere.

Nature is a kalpa-vrksha, a wish-fulfilling tree, which gives humanity all abundance. But today our situation is like that of a fool sawing off the very branch on which he is seated.

57

Even if we only have a tiny plot of land, we should try to grow a few vegetables using organic fertilisers. Spending some time with our plants, we should talk to them, kiss them and sing to them. This relationship will give us a new vitality.

58

Everyone knows that human beings cannot live in a desert. If atmospheric purification does not take place, the health of humans will deteriorate. We should grow plenty of trees and also medicinal plants, because they cleanse the air. Many diseases will be prevented if we breathe in the air that has come into contact with medicinal plants.

59

Some say that we should plant two trees for every one we cut down. But this is still inadequate. There is a great difference in what a large tree provides and what two small trees can provide. If a disinfectant is added to water in a smaller proportion than required, its effect will be minimised. If an Ayurvedic medicine needing ten different ingredients is prepared with only eight, the medicine will not have the desired effect. Likewise, when two small seedlings replace a large tree, the balance of nature is upset.

60

Ages ago, the saints and sages of India, having delved deep into their own consciousness, proclaimed that plants and trees also have feelings, and can even express these feelings to a certain extent. When we have a loving and compassionate attitude towards plants and trees, we can learn to listen and to understand them.

When the ancient sages enjoined that we should worship the trees, they were teaching the world the importance of preserving and protecting nature. Because trees have been needlessly cut down, we do not get proper rainfall during the monsoon season. Also, the temperature has increased and weather patterns are changing all over the world. Trees purify the atmosphere, absorbing the carbon dioxide we exhale. They greatly assist the harmony of nature. Even mentally worshipping and protecting the trees that bring us so much good is beneficial.

62

In order to meet the necessities of life, it is not wrong to cut down trees and collect medicinal plants from the forests. It is certainly a necessity to have a house to protect us from the rain and sun. But it is not a necessity to build a house that makes a show of our wealth and luxurious life style. Cutting down enough trees to build a house is not adharmic (unrighteous). An action becomes unrighteous when we perform it indiscriminately, without awareness.

63

At present, the biggest threat to mankind is not a third world war, but the loss of nature's harmony and our widening separation from her. We should develop the awareness of a person at gunpoint. Only then can humanity survive.

64

Plant trees. It is a blessing to do so. Trees outlive us and provide fruit and shade to coming generations. Individually, we should each make a vow to plant at least one tree a month. In a year, each person will have planted twelve trees. Together we can restore nature's beauty to the face of the world.

65

Forests are being destroyed and apartment complexes erected in their place. Many birds build nests in these complexes. If we take a close look at these nests, we will see that they have been made with wires and pieces of plastic. This is because trees are decreasing. In the future, there may be no trees at all. The birds are learning to adapt to their new environment.

66

Each family should grow trees and plants in their yard. Planting a tree is selfless service to society. Just as we enjoy the presence of trees planted by people in the past, we too should plant for the future generations. If we haven't done any selfless acts, we should plant a tree or sapling; that would be a truly selfless deed, benefiting others and ourselves.

67

Children, not a grain of the food we eat is made purely by our own effort. What comes to us in the form of food is the work of others, the bounty of nature and God's compassion. Even if we have millions of dollars, we still need food to satisfy our hunger. Can we eat money? Therefore, never eat anything without first praying with humility and gratitude.

68

Children, nature stands before us as a symbol of renunciation. Like mountains, rivers and trees, every single object in nature is teaching us lessons in selflessness. Look at a tree—it gives fruit, shade and imparts cool air. Even as it is being felled, it offers shade to the person cutting it down. Similarly, every being and organism in nature practices renunciation in some way or the other.

69

Let us take from nature only what we really need, and try to give back to some extent. Suppose two potatoes are enough to cook a dish. If we take a third potato, we are acting indiscriminately. When we take more than our share from Mother Nature, we are also denying others their share. Perhaps our neighbour, who does not have enough food, could have had a meal. Thus, when we exploit nature, we are also exploiting others.

70

When compassion arises within us, we will sincerely wish to help and protect all beings. In that state, we won't feel like plucking even a single leaf unnecessarily. To pluck ten leaves, when only five leaves are needed, is an adharmic act. We would only pick a flower on the last day of its existence, right before it falls from the stem. We would consider it very harmful to the plant if, due to our greediness, we plucked the flower on the very first day.

71

The never-ending stream of love that flows from a true believer towards the entire creation will have a gentle, soothing effect on nature. Our love is the best protection of nature.

72

The need of the hour is to cultivate a society of good-hearted individuals. As spiritual beings, we should each strive to lead a pure and straight forward life of sacrifice. A spiritual being should be like a tree that gives shade even to the person who cuts it asunder. A spiritual being should be like the wind that blows equally over both excreta and the flower.

73

You will not be admitted into the realm of God without the signature of even the smallest ant on your application. The first requirement for liberation, along with your constant remembrance of the Supreme Being, is that you love all beings, both sentient and insentient. When you attain this greatness of heart, freedom won't be far behind.

74

Anyone who has the courage to overcome the limitations of the mind will attain the state of Universal Motherhood. This is a love and compassion felt not only towards one's own child, but also towards all people, animals, plants, rocks and rivers. It is a love extended to all of nature and all beings. To one in whom the state of true motherhood has awakened, all creatures are her children. This awakening of love, this motherhood, is Divine Love. This is God.

75

Today we are aware of the need to protect Mother Earth, and of course, this is essential. But we must also be concerned with the pollution of our inner environment. Our negative thoughts and actions create pollution in the atmosphere and in the consciousness of humanity. Only through love and compassion are the protection and preservation of nature possible.

76

With the lack of values and righteous living, nature has started reacting. As the trees diminish, rain also becomes less. When the rain does come, it comes at the wrong time. It is the same with sunshine; nowadays it is either too much or too little. These are some effects of our wrong actions and attitudes.

77

Negative thoughts and actions contaminate the atmosphere and the consciousness of humanity. If we don't change our ways, we are paving the way for our own destruction. This is not a punishment but an injury we are inflicting upon ourselves. We are not making use of the gifts God has provided for us to think, discriminate, and act wisely.

78

Life becomes fulfilled when humankind and nature move together, hand in hand in harmony. When melody and rhythm complement each other, the music becomes beautiful and pleasing to the ear. Likewise, when people live in accordance with the laws of nature, life becomes like a beautiful song.

79

My children, one of our highest priorities should be to preserve nature. We must put an end to the practice of destroying the environment for money and for our selfish, short-term needs. We have no right to destroy. We cannot create; therefore, we should not destroy. Only God can create, sustain, and destroy. All three are beyond our capacity.

80

God dwells not only in human beings but also in animals and all species of life—in the mountains, rivers, valleys, and trees. In the birds, clouds, stars, sun and moon—everywhere. God dwells in "sarvacharaachara," both the moving and unmoving. How can a person who understands this kill and destroy?

81

Sincere Truth seekers and believers cannot harm nature because they see nature as God. They don't experience nature as being separate. They are the real lovers of nature. Where there is no mind or ego, you are one with the whole of existence. Children, when you are one with creation, when your heart is filled with nothing but love, all of nature will be your friend and will serve you. The universe, along with all of its beings, is your friend.

82

Looking at Mother Nature and observing her selfless way of giving, we can become aware of our own limitations. This will help us develop devotion and surrender to the Supreme Being. Nature can bring us closer to God and teach us how to truly worship the Divine.

83

Only through love and compassion is the protection and preservation of nature possible. But both these qualities are fast diminishing in human beings. In order to feel real love and compassion, one must realise the oneness of the life force that sustains and is the substratum of the entire universe.

84

Today's youth are the pillars of tomorrow's world. The young have the potential to make great change in the world. Our dedicated youth can inspire others by coming together to create initiatives to protect Mother Nature. We should channel their energy towards a good cause.

85

Earth cannot be changed for the better unless the consciousness of individuals changes first. We can pledge to increase our awareness by disciplining our minds through meditation, prayer and positive thinking. We can commit ourselves to a global ethic of understanding one another, and to socially beneficial, peace-fostering, and nature-friendly ways of life. With risk and readiness to sacrifice, there can be a fundamental change in our situation.

Meditation, prayer, chanting and other spiritual practices are our salvation. The reverence and devotion that human beings develop through their religious faith is very beneficial—both to humanity and to nature. Chanting a mantra or prayers with concentration will definitely create a positive change in nature and help restore harmony.

87

We may doubt whether we have the power to restore the lost balance in nature. We may ask, "Aren't we human beings too limited?" No, we are not! We have infinite power within us, but we are fast asleep and unaware of our own strength. This power will rise up when we awaken within.

88

A person who has become one with the Supreme Consciousness has also become one with all of creation. Such a person is no longer just the body but becomes the Life Force that shines in and through everything. He or she becomes the Consciousness that lends its beauty and vitality to everything.

89

Mahatmas (Realised Souls) can express themselves through the sun, the moon, the ocean, mountains, trees and animals—through the entire universe. When one is egoless, one is everything. The entire universe is one with an enlightened being.

90

More than knowledge of modern science, it is the deeper understanding of religion—the truth of the oneness in all creation—that teaches people to love nature and to develop a sense of reverence and devotion towards all beings. You may feel that destroying a tree or a plant is a lesser wrong than killing a human being. This concept is wrong.

91

Plants and trees also have emotions and can feel fear. When somebody approaches a tree or plant with an axe or a hacking knife, the plant is afraid; it trembles with fear. You need a subtle ear to hear its cries, a subtle eye to see its helplessness, and a subtle mind to feel its fear. You do not see its suffering, but can feel it with a compassionate heart. To see the suffering of a plant, your mind's eye must be open. Unfortunately, you do not see subtle things with your external eyes. Because of this, you destroy a helpless tree or plant.

92

When human beings make nature happy by having good thoughts and doing good actions, nature blesses us with bountiful, overflowing harvests. There is a traditional festival in Kerala called Pongal, which means 'to overflow.' This is the time when humanity's love for nature and nature's love for humanity overflow—when the universal mind and the individual mind overflow to become one.

93

When you bow down before all of existence, in utter humility, the universe bows down to you and serves you.

94

It is said that the lifespan of a butterfly is only a few days to a week. Yet how joyously it flies around! It spreads delight and happiness to everyone. Our lives should be like this.

95

There was a period of time when everybody abandoned Amma because of her unusual ways. When that happened, it was the birds and the animals who came to take care of her. One eagle would fly above her and drop fish down, which Amma would eat raw. A dog used to bring her food packets. When she came out of samadhi (a blissful state) a cow came and stood in front of her in such a position for Amma to drink as much as she wanted directly from its udders.

96

When we see Mother Nature as the embodiment of God, we will automatically serve and protect her. If we approach nature with love, it will serve us as our best friend, a friend that won't let us down.

97

My children, look at nature and imagine your Beloved Deity's form in the trees, mountains and other objects. Converse with your Beloved. Imagine your Beloved Deity standing in the sky and call out to Him or Her. Express whatever grievances you may have; why should you tell your sorrows to others?

98

It is high time to give serious thought to protecting nature. The destruction of nature is synonymous to the destruction of humanity. Trees, animals, birds, plants, forests, mountains, lakes and rivers—everything that exists in nature—is in desperate need of our kindness, compassionate care and protection. If we protect them, they in turn will protect us.

99

Nature is benefited by the concentration of spiritual people. Prayer and spiritual concentration are powerful means for purifying the atmosphere. At the same time, we can also draw spiritual power, hope and trust from being in nature—through prayer, chanting and meditation, in words or in silence.

Every small effort we make towards environmental conservation is precious because it helps to sustain life. This is actually more precious than any kind of material wealth. Through our schools, we can awaken in our children an interest in protecting nature, just like the interest we have awoken in them for amassing money.

101

In her agitation, owing to the unrighteous actions perpetrated against her by humans, Mother Nature has now begun withdrawing her blessings. It is the urgent duty of all human beings to please her by performing selfless actions endowed with mutual love, faith, and sincerity. Only then will she flow again and bless humanity with endless resources.

102

Suppose you have ten seeds. Consume nine of them if you want, but at least let one seed remain for planting. Nothing should be destroyed completely. If you receive a hundred dollars from a harvest, at least ten dollars should be given to charity.

Just as the earth moves around the sun in a regular cycle, all of nature moves in a cyclic pattern. Seasons move in a circle: spring, summer, autumn, winter, then spring again. From the seed comes the tree and the tree again provides seeds. Likewise, birth, childhood, youth, old age, death, and birth again. It is a continuous cycle. Time moves in a circle, not in a straight line. Karma and its results must inevitably be experienced by every living being until the mind is stilled and one is content in one's own Self.

104

Look at the fresh roses. How beautiful they are. What a fine fragrance they exude. But what do we give them to make them grow? Just a little used tea leaves and cow dung! What a vast difference between these beautiful flowers and the manure given to them. Likewise, impediments in our lives are the fertiliser which makes us grow stronger spiritually. These obstacles will help our hearts to blossom fully.

105

Always remember that when dusk arrives, it already has dawn in its womb.

106

We must remember that everything is sentient; everything is full of consciousness and life. Everything exists in God. There is no such thing as mere matter; consciousness alone exists. If we approach all situations with this attitude, destruction becomes impossible for us; the very idea of destruction disappears. Everything exists in God.

107

Children, Divine Love is our real nature. Love is shining in each and every one of us. There cannot be any manifestation of any kind without this power of love behind it.

108

Oh Divine Spirit, do You see me here? May Your starry hands shower grace upon me, giving me the strength to keep remembering You and the sorrow to keep calling You. You are my only refuge and comfort. Blissful and beautiful is Your Divine World! Lift me to Your world of a million twinkling stars!

www.ingramcontent.com/pod-product-compliance
Lightning Source LLC
Chambersburg PA
CBHW070614050426
42450CB00011B/3054